EXTREME JOBS

Stunt Performers

Tony Hyland

A⁺

This edition first published in 2006 in the United States of America by Smart Apple Media.

Smart Apple Media
2140 Howard Drive West
North Mankato
Minnesota 56003

First published in 2005 by
MACMILLAN EDUCATION AUSTRALIA PTY LTD
627 Chapel Street, South Yarra, Australia 3141

Visit our website at www.macmillan.com.au

Associated companies and representatives throughout the world.

Library of Congress Cataloging-in-Publication Data

Hyland, Tony.
    Stunt performers / by Tony Hyland.
    p. cm. – (Extreme jobs)
    Includes index.
    ISBN-13: 978-1-58340-739-4
    1. Stunt performers–Juvenile literature. 2. Stunt performers–Vocational guidance–Juvenile literature. I. Title.

    PN1995.9.S7H95 2006
    791.4302'8–dc22   2005057879

Edited by Ruth Jelley
Text and cover design by Peter Shaw
Page layout by SPG
Photo research by Legend Images

Printed in USA

Acknowledgments
The author is grateful for the assistance provided by Ringling Brothers and Barnum and Bailey Circus and Cirque du Soleil in arranging interviews for this book.
The author and the publisher are grateful to the following for permission to reproduce copyright material:

Cover photograph: Performance by Cirque Du Soleil's "Varekai" courtesy of Kevin Winter/Getty Images

AAP/EPA/Jonathan Drake, p. 10; Australian Picture Library/Corbis, pp. 5, 15, 18, 22, 23; © Cirque du Soleil Inc, photo: Mark Ashman, p. 25 (Lance Trappe); photo: Véronique Vial, costume: Dominique Lemieux, p. 25 (Cycles Act from La Nouba™ by Cirque du Soliel®); The Flying Wallendas, p. 29; Getty Images, pp. 9, 30; Peter Brandt/Getty Images, p. 6; Ken Goff/Time Life Pictures/Getty Images, p. 19; Hulton Archive/Getty Images, p. 13; MGM Studios/Getty Images, p. 12; Kevin Winter/Getty Images, pp. 1, 24; Peter Hassall, photo by Craig Voisin, pp. 8, 16; Chris Kemp, p. 17 top; Lee Howell Photography 2004, p. 17 bottom; Photolibrary.com, pp. 7, 26; Photolibrary.com/IndexStock, p. 28; Picture Media/Reuters/Carlos Barria, p. 11; Picture Media/Reuters/Chip East, pp. 20, 21; Picture Media/Reuters/Oleg Popov, p. 14; Ringling Bros. and Barnum & Bailey, pp. 4, 27 (both).

Contents

Glossary words
When a word is printed in **bold**, you can look up its meaning in the Glossary on page 31.

Do you want to be a stunt performer?

Could you be a stunt performer, performing spectacular stunts in front of an audience or movie camera?

Stunt performers perform aerial acrobatics in circuses, or dangerous stunts for the movies. Circus performers can swing on the flying trapeze high above the audience. Stunt actors can crash speeding cars in movie stunts.

We all love watching exciting stunts. Most people will enjoy the show and go home. For the stunt performers, this is the day's work. They'll be back doing more spectacular stunts the following day.

Stunt work is an extreme job. The training is hard and the stunts can be dangerous. But performers enjoy the thrill of their work and push themselves hard to do more spectacular stunts.

Perhaps you could be a stunt performer one day.

Trapeze artists perform spectacular stunts high up in the big top.

Stunt actor or circus performer?

Stunt actors work in movies and television shows. They work hard to make it look as if someone else is doing the stunt. Circus performers work just as hard to be the stars of the show.

Stunt actors dressed up as the stars in a movie do all the dangerous and difficult scenes. Movie scenes can be **edited** to cut out some parts and put others in. Film crews can take hours to shoot an action scene. The audience only sees a few exciting moments.

Circus artists perform spectacular stunts live, in front of an audience. If the stunt goes wrong, there is no chance to do it again.

EXTREME INFO

Car chases

Car chase scenes are fun to watch, but not easy to make. Streets are blocked off and the stunt actors work out exactly how the scene will work before the action begins.

Stunt actors work with the stunt and film crews.

Life as a stunt performer

Stunt actors lead a busy and energetic life. They must be fit and strong. Many start off in **martial arts** or **gymnastics**, where they learn to develop flexibility and fall safely.

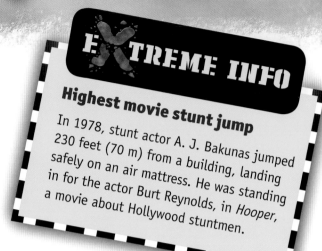

Experienced stunt actors learn many extra skills such as horse riding, working with explosives, and scuba diving. Some become specialists in one skill, such as stunt driving.

Stunt actors work wherever movies or television shows are made. Hollywood is known as the movie capital of the world. Other places with busy movie or television studios include Vancouver in Canada, and Queensland in Australia. Stunt actors often work **on location**. This means filming in remote places such as deserts, jungles, and mountains. Stunt actors working on these jobs are away from home for weeks, or even months.

Stunt actors often have to work in faraway places.

Circus life

Circus life is also busy and active. Performers need to be strong and agile. They need a good sense of balance and a head for heights. The circus is not a place for shy people; circus performers enjoy being the center of attention. Most circus acts are performed to music. The rhythm of the music gives the performers cues for each section of their act.

Many circuses travel from town to town. They stay for a week, and then move on. Circus performers are used to this traveling life. Many have no other home but the circus. They live

Circus performers travel around the country, performing spectacular stunts.

in large caravans or trailers. Circus families often travel together, with the children learning to join their parents' act. Circus children don't usually go to school. They study by **correspondence**, or have a teacher who travels with the circus.

Risks and dangers

Stunt performers of all types know that their jobs are risky. They don't let the risks stop them. Their skills and training usually keep them safe. Some of the risks for stunt performers are:

Falls
Stunt performers are used to falls, and know how to land safely. But a fall from the highwire or trapeze can be deadly.

Sports injuries
Stunt performers are hard on their bodies. They often suffer exactly the same sprains and knee damage that sports stars do.

Fire and explosions
Movie fires and explosions are spectacular, but if something goes wrong, stunt actors can be badly hurt.

Accidents
A slight miscalculation, or a piece of damaged equipment, can cause a bad accident. That's why performers practice their stunts and check their equipment closely.

Bad weather
Wind and rain on a movie set can create unexpected hazards for stunt actors.

Stunt performers learn how to do falls and flips safely.

Fire!

Movie scripts sometimes call for a character to catch fire. This is a very dangerous task, which only experienced stunt actors will perform. Thick layers of protective cream are smeared all over the stunt actor's skin. The actor wears several layers of long underwear soaked in **protective gel**. A protective mask keeps flames away from the actor's face. Finally, the actor wears normal clothes, which are set on fire using a special **fire gel**.

The **stunt crew** stand just out of the camera's view, ready with fire extinguishers. As soon as the shot is finished, they rush in and douse the fire. The movie audience will see a scene of a burning figure running or jumping through flames. But they won't see the careful preparations that went on behind the scenes.

EXTREME INFO

Fire

Fire stunts don't always go right. Stunt actors have been badly burned when they tripped, or when a sudden gust of wind fanned the flames on their clothing.

Only experienced stunt actors perform fire stunts.

9

Training

Stunt actors train in a wide range of skills. They often start with martial arts but they also learn several other sports. They also train in areas such as driving, horse riding, scuba diving, skydiving, and mountain climbing.

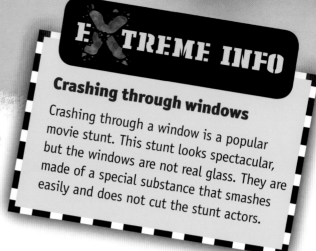

EXTREME INFO

Crashing through windows

Crashing through a window is a popular movie stunt. This stunt looks spectacular, but the windows are not real glass. They are made of a special substance that smashes easily and does not cut the stunt actors.

Experienced stunt actors sometimes run stunt classes. Here, students can learn how to fake fights, fall down stairs, and work with fire. First aid training is essential for stunt actors, in case of accidents on the set.

Working stunt actors need to keep their skills and fitness levels high. They work out in the gym and practice skills such as falling and horse riding.

Martial arts provides good training for stunt actors.

Learning circus skills

Many circus performers first learned their skills when they were children, as their parents were also performers. They learn trapeze and highwire skills as they travel around the country with the circus.

However, you don't have to come from a circus family to learn circus skills. There are circus classes in many cities where even young children can learn circus acts. Some students go on to become famous circus performers. Other circus performers start off learning gymnastics or calisthenics. These classes teach students to be strong, yet graceful and artistic. Students also learn how to put together an exciting performance for their audience.

Experienced circus performers practice for hours each day. They need to be fit and strong. Their **routines** must look smooth and skillful.

Circus performers practice their routines every day.

EXTREME INFO

Circus kids

The Flying Fruit Fly Circus is a famous Australian children's circus that started off as an after-school class. The performers are aged from 8 to 18 years, and perform shows all over the world.

Stunts in history

People have enjoyed watching stunt performers for thousands of years. Ancient Roman circuses had chariot races and bareback horse riders. They also had deadly fights with gladiators and wild animals.

About 1,000 to 1,500 years ago, acrobats and jugglers strolled from town to town, performing in the streets. Modern circuses started in England in the 1700s. Soon, the idea spread to Europe and America. The circuses were small and made up of riding acts, jugglers, and clowns.

In the late 1800s, huge traveling circuses appeared in America. They toured from town to town in circus trains, putting on their show in a large tent called the big top. Companies such as Ringling Brothers and Barnum and Bailey competed to put on the biggest, most spectacular shows.

The ancient Romans enjoyed wild chariot races at their circus.

Stunts at the movies

The first silent movies were made in the early 1900s. Movie directors soon realized that with clever editing and special effects, they could make almost any action look real.

The first stunt actors appeared in battle scenes, car crashes, and train wrecks. Stunt experts learned how to make crashes appear more and more spectacular. Many of today's stunts, such as smashing windows and breaking furniture, were invented for the silent movies by stunt actors. Because the movies were silent, actors couldn't tell jokes. Comedy movies relied on **slapstick humor**. Audiences would always laugh when someone received a pie in their face, or when too many people tried to pack themselves into the one car. Stunt actors made falls and crashes look hilarious.

The Keystone Kops used slapstick humor in silent movies to entertain audiences.

EXTREME INFO

Harold Lloyd

Harold Lloyd was famous for stunts such as dangling from a clock tower, looking as though he was hanging on for dear life.

Stunt jobs

Stunt actors

Stunt actors take the place of the real actors whenever there are any dangerous scenes. Even simple jobs like riding a bike or skateboard are usually passed on to the stunt actors.

Stunt actors begin their career doing simple background action and group fight scenes. During this time, they learn how to be part of a stunt crew and practice new skills. After about two years, they can start doing close-up stunts and progress to more difficult stunts, such as working with fire.

Stunt actors need to be ready for any job. In the space of a week they could be riding horses, falling off a building, and fighting with swords.

A stunt actor performs for a film crew.

Stunt drivers

Stunt drivers do high-speed racing, crashing and rolling cars and motorbikes. They do advanced driver training, learning to drive and stop safely at high speeds.

Stunt crews prepare crashing or rolling stunts carefully. A steel roll cage is fitted inside the car, to protect the driver. The fuel tank is removed and replaced with a smaller tank, to reduce the fire risk. The driver wears protective clothing. Drivers roll a car by running two wheels on a ramp, which is hidden from the camera.

Stunt drivers do more than just crash cars. Often they need to drive through tight places at high speed. Many car commercials use **precision drivers**, who perform spectacular stunts without damaging the cars.

RISK FACTOR

Stunt drivers are skillful, but there are risks in the work they do, such as:

- fires
- accidents caused by misjudging speed
- wet or oily road surfaces

Expert stunt actors can make car crash stunts look spectacular.

15

Stunt jobs

Fight choreographers

Just as dances are choreographed, stunt performances are also choreographed. Fight choreographers plan each step of fight scenes.

Fight choreographers are experts in martial arts and using weapons, such as swords. With the film crew, they decide how the stunt actors will move across the set, and which **props** they will need. Fight choreographers must explain things clearly. The actors, stunt crew, and film crew all need to understand how the scene will work.

Stunt actors learn to kick and punch without hurting each other. They practice each blow in slow motion. Props such as chairs and tables are made of light materials that break with little effort. Later, sound effects are added to make the fight sound real.

EXTREME INFO

When things go wrong

Fight scenes are carefully planned, but things can go wrong and stunt actors can get injured. The stunt crew is always ready to treat any injuries.

Stunt actors carefully practice a fight scene.

PROFILE

Chris Kemp

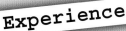

Chris Kemp has been a stunt actor for over ten years.

Stunt actor

Job

I'm a stunt actor for movies, television shows, and commercials. I do driving stunts, falls, horse riding, and water work.

Experience

I trained in martial arts, and I've been working as a stunt actor for over ten years. I'm also a scuba **dive master** and a fire specialist.

Career highlight

Working in fight scenes with martial arts actor, Jackie Chan.

Scariest moment

I was working with a crew in rough weather, in a movie about navy commandos. We were supposed to come ashore in an inflatable boat, but a wave flipped us over.

What I don't like

Working under extreme conditions, when it is very hot or very cold. Once, I was playing a dead body floating in cold water. They had to reshoot the scene several times, and I got **hypothermia**.

Why I do this job

I love the physical challenge. I enjoy knowing how to do a fall, or how to make a fight look violent, and yet not get hurt.

Chris Kemp performs a stunt for a television commercial.

Stunt jobs

Stunt coordinators

Stunts need to be prepared carefully. This is the job of the stunt coordinator. Stunt coordinators are expert stunt actors. They understand the risks and know how the stunts can be performed safely.

Stunt coordinators work with the film crew and the director. They decide what stunts the movie needs. Then they find the best stunt actors for the job. Stunt coordinators plan every detail, making sure that the stunts are done safely. Most stunts need special equipment, such as explosives, safety harnesses, or fake weapons. The stunt coordinators make sure that this equipment is in good working order. The director, camera crew, actors, and stunt crew all work together to make a stunt happen correctly.

Stunt coordinators work with the film crew to plan every detail of a stunt.

Second-unit directors

A second-unit director is a stunt expert in charge of filming all of the stunts for a movie.

While the main film crew works in the studio with the stars, the second-unit crew films the stunts. Later, film editors join all of the sections together so that the action seems to flow smoothly.

Second-unit directors take charge of a large and expensive operation. They work with the director to decide exactly how the stunts will fit in with the story. They also have control over costumers, lighting and camera people, as well as the stunt crew. Battle scenes in movies can use hundreds of stunt actors and extras. All over the battlefield, soldiers fight and explosions go off. This is no time for mistakes. Mistakes can waste hours of time, and cost enormous amounts of money, especially for movie battle scenes with hundreds of people to be paid.

Second-unit directors coordinate large stunts, such as battle scenes.

19

Stunt jobs

Daredevils

EXTREME INFO

Leaping Snake Canyon

When daredevil Evel Knievel tried to jump a motorbike across Snake Canyon in 1974, he didn't make it. His rocket-propelled motorcycle took off from a special ramp, but his parachute opened too early and he crashed into the river below.

Crowds love to see daredevils in action. Whether it is Blondin walking a tightrope across Niagara Falls or Evel Knievel leaping a motorbike across Snake Canyon, crowds are eager to watch.

Daredevils are different than stunt actors. The name "daredevil" is used for performers who put on shows in front of huge crowds. Modern daredevils usually drive stunt cars or motorbikes. They race through fire, or fly over rows of cars and trucks.

Daredevil acts are designed to look both spectacular and dangerous. The performer often wears a bright and colorful costume. Loud music and bright lights create an exciting atmosphere.

Daredevil costumes are bright and spectacular.

Behind the daredevil stunts

Daredevil performers usually travel with a stunt crew. Unseen by the audience, the crew takes careful precautions in setting up the stunts. Motorbikes have powerful engines and special tires fitted. The daredevil's costume might be colorful, but it is designed for safety. It includes a strong helmet, leather boots, and fireproof clothing.

Stunt crew members plan every aspect of the stunt, to make sure it can be done safely. They check the equipment to make sure it is in top condition. When it's time for the big show, the stunt crew will be ready. If everything goes well, they breathe a sigh of relief. But if things go badly, they are ready with fire extinguishers and first aid equipment!

RISK FACTOR

Daredevils enjoy putting on a show, but they face risks, such as:

- misjudging speed
- misjudging the angle of approach
- wet weather, which can make surfaces slippery

The stunt crew cannot be seen by the crowd while the daredevil performs his stunt.

60

AVP

Stunt jobs

Acrobats and jugglers

Acrobats and jugglers are traditional circus performers. They need very little equipment, and rely on their own physical strength and agility.

Acrobats often work in pairs or teams. They jump, leap, and twist, balancing on equipment or even on top of each other. The strongest member is the catcher. Two or more acrobats balance on the catcher's shoulders.

Acrobats use many of the skills that gymnasts use. They need to be very strong and agile. Acrobats use simple props such as kitchen chairs, balancing several on top of each other, sometimes with one person on top of the pile. Springboards and mini-trampolines give an extra spring, sending the acrobats high into the air.

Acrobats leap into action, balancing on each other's shoulders.

Juggling with danger

Circus jugglers perform difficult and sometimes dangerous stunts.

Juggling is easier when all the items are the same size and weight. The jugglers can toss each item with the same force, knowing that it will return smoothly. A set of balls or clubs is easy for professional jugglers to work with. Jugglers can build up to more and more elaborate items as the act progresses. Soon, flaming torches or dangerous-looking swords might be flying through the air.

The most difficult trick is to juggle several items of different size and weight. The juggler has to judge each piece and throw it at the correct moment, or everything will come crashing down.

RISK FACTOR

Acrobats and jugglers perform tricks that need excellent balance. Some of the risks they face are:

- falls caused by human error
- over-confidence
- misjudging a throw or jump
- sports injuries, such as damaged knees or shoulders

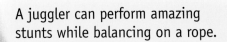

A juggler can perform amazing stunts while balancing on a rope.

Stunt jobs

Modern circus performers

EXTREME INFO

Underwater secrets

In the *Cirque du Soleil* water circus, performers disappear underwater, then appear a few minutes later. The audience cannot see the scuba divers at the bottom of the tank, who supply air to the performers and lead them to where they reappear.

Modern circus performers do stunning and elegant aerial routines. Their acts blend together to tell a story. The performers wear elaborate costumes and make-up, moving in time to mysterious rhythms.

Traditional circuses are loud, noisy, and fun. Modern circuses are often quiet and mysterious, but just as much fun. Modern circuses such as Canada's *Cirque du Soleil*, and Australia's Circus Oz were started by the performers themselves. They wanted to do shows that were like a theatre performance, rather than just a string of circus acts.

Cirque du Soleil sends troupes of performers all over the world. It also has permanent circuses in many cities.

Cirque du Soleil performers wear spectacular costumes and perform elegant routines.

PROFILE

Lance Trappe
Bike stunt performer

Lance Trappe performs in *La Nouba*.

Job

I'm a bike stunt performer in the *Cirque du Soleil* show *La Nouba*, at Disney World in Florida.

Experience

I competed professionally for eight years on the world's number one mountain bike team. I was a U.S. team member at the world championships twice.

My Work

The most challenging part is applying my theatrical make-up before the show! It takes about an hour. Then I put on my pads, costume, gloves, and helmet. I check over my bike and warm up, waiting for the lift to bring me up onto the stage. Once I'm on stage, I ride non-stop for several action-packed minutes, until I make my exit and the performance is over.

Risks

My performance is potentially risky. As long as I keep my skills sharp and my body in shape, everything is under control. At *Cirque du Soleil* I have access to any training or practice time I need.

Lance Trappe does a spectacular bike stunt.

Stunt jobs

Aerial artists

Aerial artists of many kinds perform in circuses. They soar and fly high above the heads of the audience.

EXTREME INFO

Get your teeth into this

Some aerial artists hang by their teeth! They use a swiveling mouthpiece, attached to a cable. They spin and twist, but their hands never touch the cable.

Flying trapeze artists swing and leap, doing amazing double somersaults. Like acrobats, trapeze teams usually include a strong catcher. Lighter members of the team do twists and somersaults as the catcher swings in to catch them. **Lyra** artists perform gracefully as the cable pulls the lyra to the roof, or swings it around the circus ring. **Chiffon** performers swing on a long strip of brightly colored fabric hanging from the roof. They wrap the chiffon around their legs or bodies as they go. They don't use a net or safety harness. They rely on their muscles and the strong fabric to hold them.

The performer is supported by the chiffon fabric.

Sylvia Zerbini

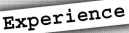

Sylvia Zerbini comes from a long family line of circus performers.

Aerial artist

Job

I'm an aerial artist with Ringling Brothers and Barnum and Bailey Circus. I perform on the trapeze and the lyra.

Experience

My parents were circus performers, and I grew up in the circus environment. I did my first solo trapeze act when I was 13 years old.

My act

I combine a lyra act with my eight Arabian and Andalusian horses. I ride the horses around the ring, then catch the lyra and soar into the air.

Things can go wrong

Once I slipped from a trapeze bar. I tried to catch the bar again, but missed and fell to the ground. Fortunately, I was not badly hurt.

Why I do this

Aerial work gives me a feeling that I don't experience anywhere else. When I'm 49 feet (15 m) in the air and doing a freefall, I get to block everything else out.

Sylvia Zerbini directs her circus horses while hanging from the lyra.

Stunt jobs

Highwire performers

Highwire performers seem to be doing the impossible. They walk, run, and leap on a wire no thicker than a child's thumb.

Highwire performers have an amazing sense of balance. They need to be very strong and athletic. They dance around, balance on each other's shoulders, and even do handstands on top of chairs. Most people couldn't even do that on the ground.

One secret of highwire performing is the way the **rigging** is set up. The wire is pulled very tight and hard, so that it cannot sway or bounce.

Highwire performers can even ride a bike on the highwire!

EXTREME INFO

Wire bouncing

Highwire performers bounce onto each other's shoulders high above the crowd. They balance a mini-trampoline in the middle of the highwire. The star performer jumps from one person's shoulders on to the trampoline, then bounces on to a third performer's shoulders!

The Flying Wallendas

The famous Wallenda family have been performing in circuses for many years. Their most spectacular highwire stunt is the seven-person pyramid. The performers walk the tightrope, balancing on each other's shoulders. They never use a net!

The Flying Wallendas perform a seven-person pyramid without a net.

The Wallenda family traveled around the U.S. performing their show. In 1962, the pyramid collapsed. Two performers were killed and one was paralyzed. The others managed to cling to the wire until they could be rescued. In 1978, the family leader, Karl Wallenda, died when he fell from a wire that was not rigged correctly.

Today, members of the Wallenda family still perform the seven-person pyramid. Once, they even formed a ten-person pyramid for a television show.

RISK FACTOR

Highwire walkers usually work with a net, but their performance is very risky. They must deal with:

- accidents caused by overbalancing
- faulty equipment
- poorly rigged ropes and wires

Could you perform stunts?

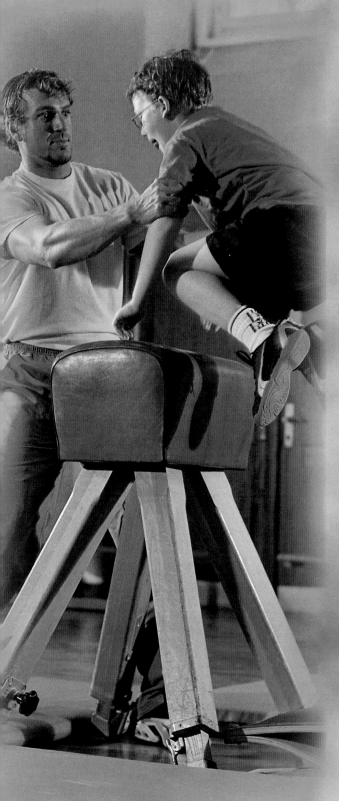

You could be a stunt performer if you:

- have normal health

- are very fit

- have a good sense of balance

- are good at activities such as gymnastics or martial arts

- enjoy being physically active

- are not afraid of heights

If you learn martial arts such as judo or karate, you could become a movie stunt actor. If you prefer circus work, you could learn gymnastics or calisthenics, or go to circus classes.

Try a gymnastics or martial arts class—you'll have fun, and it's a good way to see if stunt work will suit you.

Perhaps you could be a stunt performer one day.

Glossary

chiffon	brightly colored fabric used in aerial circus performances
correspondence	system of teaching by mail
dive master	qualified and experienced scuba diver
edited	have sections of film put together
fire gel	a Jell-O-like substance which burns with large flames
gymnastics	a sport which develops strength and agility
harness	sets of strong straps worn around the hips that can be attached to safety cables
hypothermia	a condition where the body temperature is dangerously low
lyra	a suspended steel hoop used in circus acts
martial arts	self-defense sports such as judo and karate
on location	filming a movie away from the studio
precision drivers	drivers who perform accurate driving stunts at high speed
props	items used in stunts, such as fake weapons and furniture
protective gel	a water-based Jell-O-like substance which protects against burns
rigging	ropes and cables used to support the highwire
routines	the sets of actions and movements performed in stunt acts
slapstick humor	lively physical comedy used by clowns or in silent movies
stunt crew	team of stunt actors who set up and perform stunts

Index